prisoner

linda pyke

prisoner

macmillan of canada / toronto

Canadian Cataloguing in Publication Data

Pyke, Linda, 1948-
   Prisoner

Poems.

ISBN 0-7705-1715-3

I. Title.

PS8581.Y44P75   C811'.5'4   C78-001231-3
PR9199.3.P94P75

Design and production art
Dreadnaught Toronto

*Cover and frontispiece photo courtesy of
Montreal Star / Canada Wide*

Printed in Canada for
The Macmillan Company of Canada Limited
70 Bond Street, Toronto
M5B 1X3

I wish to acknowledge for her continual love and
encouragement my mother,
Anne Pyke (1916–1978).

Excerpts from *prisoner* have appeared in:
The Antigonish Review
The Canadian Forum
The Dalhousie Review
The Malahat Review
Prism International
Quarry
Revue 2
The Tamarack Review
Waves
and have been broadcast on the CBC radio arts program "Anthology".

for edmund

contents

giver of life
taker of life
i must not confuse you with god

the captive prince

i

the bars, concrete,
and the years,

barriers of time
and space:

over there,
the sentinels,
rifles erect
and ready,

the courtyard,
shadowed
towards evening,

the high wall.

ii

under what strange spell
have you fallen?

you walk in a waking
dream /
        you sleep
and dream of freedom.

2

iii

of course,
you are guilty

(you do not deny),

but you bear
a universal guilt,

the crime becomes
almost irrelevant.

iv

we meet
through devious means:

my poem in a magazine,
your letter.

and now we write back and forth
sooner and sooner as if somehow
this ritual exchange of photographs
and books life histories and poems
could help us transcend touch
one the other

v

and having never touched,
we are lovers.

i take courage
from héloïse and abélard,

but on their side
was god,

we have only eros.

vi

and eros is enough.

vii

sitting upon this chair
(a throne, subtle
instrument of torture):

the arms are your arms,
the seat, your lap,

4

you contain me
as i, you,

very deep and still,

i am impaled.

viii

and i rock your head
between my thighs,
come to your fingertips,

you become past,
present, future,

everyman /
                your face.

ix

and nights
in dreams (yours, mine)
i visit your cell,

5

i come to that narrow,
celibate bed,

fall upon you
trembling,
hair long and golden,
tumbling,

we are enclosed
in light:

open
        as i open,

we enter other realms.

6

the crime

men have murdered before
and for less
                    or more
than this
ancient crime
                    against property,
this trespassing
                    upon woman-flesh,

(i do not minimize):

he found the opening
between her thighs,
and you, compelled
to act,

and if you knew anything
at that moment
                    (hollow voices,
                    blurring room,
                    electric colours,
                    your blood's
low hum),
you knew you were revenge,
death
                    as in the tarot pack
or in a bergman film.

and it did not end
                    here
with fatal blow, with acid-
vision ceasing:

knife arcs through air
steel door slides closed

and still, the slow unreeling.

portrait of a lady

your lady, tossing back
her long, black hair,
impassive as the mona lisa,
and tilting two perfect
sixteen-year-old breasts
at the jury, mostly male,
must have been impressive:
i suppose they did not notice
her poor grammar
(i seen this,
        he done that),
were more intrigued
by the geometry of 3
in a bed, and thighs
sheathed in deep sky blue,
and when she told them
how she'd led the police
to the place
you discarded the knife,
they decided
her heart was the standard gold.

odyssey

like penelope,
i wait,
retain my faith:
how many years,
this body, to resist
and ache.

your ship has steered
its confident course
to vietnam, the orient,
and then south
where stretch of sea
meets stretch of sky,
uninterrupted blue,
harmony and peace.

in '67 arriving
at california coast,
lured by ladies
on the beach,
(die lorelei in denim),
confronting manson,
mythic creature,
face to face.

san francisco:
brief blue movie career,
the woman and the room,
photographer, an acrobat,
his one unblinking eye
(i long to view the film).

and the summer
melting into years,
good music /
                better dope,
women and a place to crash,
the wilderness,
                the street,
trip went on and on . . .

till north to gastown, canada,
the fatal mistake,
further journeys aborted:

the prison years,
i wait.

southern boy

1948: they fished me
from my mother's belly,
cut the cord,
while you were down
in north carolina,
8 years old,
character quite formed.
you were casting
your line far into the centre
of some hidden swamp,
skipping school,
and dreaming the day
never-ending,
remembering
the wages of sin.
and you were a pretty one
— weren't you? —
blue-gold eyes,
sunbleached hair,
and a voice heavy
and slow as the scent
of magnolia blossoms'
late-unfurling.
no wonder she was eager:
        girl cousin /
            boy cousin,
        failed connection,
        caught and beaten again . . .

ah, but one steamy day
we'll replay the scene,
sneak under a stranger's porch,
you can cup my ass
in your fisherman hands,
cast long and deep,
need never go home.

expatriate

you are unimpressed
with us,
you have it all
                reversed:

crossing the border,
as through a mirror,
you found chaos,
not peace . . .

would it help you
if i told you
draft dodgers
have found solace here,
transplanted managers,
pedestrian professors?

canada is a nice place
for the inactive and the bland,

you were just too much for us,
we could not supply
what you had to demand.

still, it's not our fault
you broke the law,
were sent to prison:
        our laws are logical,
        our prisons, clean.

but now you're always cold
and lonely here,
out of your element
among our books and thought.

you claim even the worst
in america at least
has substance,
in america with certainty
one can hate.

methods

how fortunate
it was 1971 not 1791
when you'd have been assigned
a cell in the walnut street jail
they gave you a bed
and a bible
just you and god
in that essential space

                         the struggle

it is said that men
went mad and died
in solitary
incanting revelations
strings of begats
their penitence unproven

en route to kingston

you were thinking
this is the city
of my love
you were thinking

and outside the window
snow
blurring the trees
        office buildings
        apartment towers

so you could not see

and the plane touching down
just beyond

and the long stark corridors
of terminal two
(our airports like prisons
our hospitals and schools)

and you were led brusquely
close-tethered
close-guarded
a dangerous force untamed

you were thinking
of a poem

of a face beneath yours
in a room in a building
unseen

and the white snow swirling
and the face calm sleeping
the dream   the ache
and the promise

welcoming

the first sight you see,
turning in the drive
(busload of new convicts,
wearing chains of passage):
at the edge
            of the highway,
wedge of land,
20 tombstones,
deliberately arranged,
20 tombstones,
20 men unclaimed.

the climate is fair today,
ontario, friendly
with fields of corn,
some horses, cows,
a prison, graveyard,
bus.

visiting day

remember the film?

bette davis to sing sing,
a moll to her lover,
cigarette
between red lips,
platinum hair
and kohl-black eyes,
part of the role
of loving a bad man,
to seem hard,
unafraid.

and i come to you,
proceed through gates,
bolted doors,
corridors echoing,
concrete underfoot.

the guards,
        impartial eyes,

purse searched,
        pockets,
         for some instrument
crude and lethal.

      (all i hide
      is my body,
      all i bring
      is my warmth.)

and i come to you,

brief kiss,
hands touch,
all words overheard.

sunday tea

kingston is a city
of many big houses,

but the big house
i approach
has no circular drive,
no hedges, flowers,
ancient stone:

instead it stands,
jumble of connected
building blocks
(white and blue),
the barren field,
wire fence enclosure,

and at tea-time,
we drink
from paper cups,

our servants carry guns.

22

visiting room

i've heard the rumour
that god is for everyone
including sinners,
if one believes in sin,
and yet, i was amazed:

gazing upward, bound for bliss
(your hand in my skirt),
suddenly i saw the light
shafting in through stained glass,
simple motif: blue, green, yellow,
and then, the arching roof,
like countless ribs or bars,
i was afraid.

consider those rural,
ontario men and women,
weary on sundays, come to pray,
consider their parson
knew them all by name,
blessed them into the world and out,
blessed their unions, reunions,
their new-born, their still-born,
blessed, most of all, their land . . .

and he stood then,
where guards stand now,

your hand in my skirt,
ancient ghosts,
the shadow and the light.

crime and punishment

this logic is seductive.

i seek to know you,
i compare:

barrow
       barabbas
              abélard
rasputin
       starkweather
              harris
raskolnikov
              i could go on . . .

i gather names
into a liturgy
of sinners, saints,
men of crime and passion,

i rewrite your history
again and again,
i am always the woman:

bonnie parker,
tough-talking, gun-toting,
master mind,

héloïse
at midnight letters,

alexandra mesmerized,

caril ann fugate,
romantic and ripe
(for the alchemy
of semen and blood),

and the women who wait,
some faithful, some not,
while punishment endured.

faces/photographs

i

beyond your window,
a blur of years,
continually shifting
angles of light,

and in the glass,
features softening,
lines traced
around eyes, mouth . . .

and you still look like
gable, like your father,
like my father.

(change is merely optical
illusion,
depending on setting
and mood.)

ii

of course there was a time
i had not seen your face:

27

all i knew were words
strung along a page,
the patient rhythm
of your hand,
moving left to right.

i constructed a face
of words and rhythm,

i learned to love.

iii

barrett
to your browning,

i reversed the roles:

i came to you,
and breathed life in.

iv

you stand static
before a stucco house,
          static
between two women,

28

the women are young
and tanned
because it is california,

your hat shades your eyes,

the women are smiling,
each believes you are hers
and forever,

i keep this photograph
in my living room,
and visible:

i am warned.

v

the analyst is pleased
you resemble my (dead) father,
the pieces snap into place.

i haven't the heart to tell her
she works the wrong puzzle.

vi

family day at the prison:

we go outside,
there is food and music,

we lie between blankets
(august sudden spell
of cold), someone
takes our picture.

finally i have proof.

vii

no one has seen you
or us together,
not even my mother.

i thrust it before her,
i am proud.

she says:

"no, this is not he,
not my dead husband,
not your father,
you've forgotten . . ."

she says:

"but, you are here,
as you are
in our old album,
blurred
and happy as a child."

on the map

you know where you are
rationally
on the map
on the outskirts of kingston
and north of the lake
(flat and watery and blue)

and you see where you are
on the evening news
in the weekend star
from my careless
                assuming letters

and where have you been
but our courtrooms
and prisons

for the rest
                must rely on reports

and a car on the highway
and a plane overhead

this is neither a trick
                nor a dream

impressions: family day # 2

gymnasium lights
glaring overhead,
non-magic realism,
overexposure:

green walls,
        green uniforms,
bare, white arms,
smoke hanging thick
in windowless space,
half-hearted couples dance,

and onstage: rock band
subversive
rhythms,

finally fade to black.

and later still,
one off-key voice,
knife-sharp, nostalgia
haunting:

"country roads
        take me home . . ."

for every ache
        a song.

the trip

it is a slow climb,
this roller-
                coaster
ride to you, a self-
perpetuating cycle,
one visit leading
to another,
one visit never enough.

in the van today,
i know i'm wired,
your addict,
hooked on a promise,

or worse,

one of those laboratory
rats, imprisoned,
conditioned
to lever-pressing,
remote-control
masturbation

(some even die that way
— of exhaustion).

in the van today,
haunches pressed

to leather,
as we climb,
i am a seismograph,
record the slightest
tremor,

and i know when i
arrive, hovering
at the peak,
i know that first
kiss before hello,
before we speak,
will send me hurtling
over the edge,

too soon, the swift
descent.

see how this skirt

see how this skirt
buttons
down the front

at regular
intervals
parted cloth

5 years

you have not touched
a woman

here

this act is forbidden
and therefore
sweet and ripe

till now

i have not known
the agony of pleasure
withheld

till now

the agony of pleasure

36

(there are rules
and yes they watch)

come

secretive
as adolescents

innocence
first taste of guilt

directions

and do you dream
of sapphic orgies
and i
the starring role

the setting   woods
reflecting lake
music reedy
filtered light
action and reaction

we are many
soft our rhythm
tangled hair
flesh interplay

and you aspiring
to director
within your cell
you plot our course:

> *love the ladies*
> *that i send you*
>
> *fuck them well*
> *for one who can't*

my tender master
counterpart
how insidious your spell

women most cruel

women most cruel
you love the best:
raven, cocaine vampiress,
eyes intimate
with sex and death,
hard and cool as steel.

her body was the route
you took,
her body led you in,
her silence filled the space
and soothed,
the lady smoothed
                    her perfect face,
and turned towards the moon.

it was a dream /
                    it was a dance,
the lady promised you no end . . .

. . . till passion ended everything:
betrayal in a court of law,
the aftermath of blood.

6 prison years
of hate and love,
you tell yourself familiar lies,
make shallow women mystery,
and hardness, a defence.

now in some disco, in the city,
she sits and strokes her glass
(her black-lined eyes,
                    her parted lips,
that gaze, remote yet beckoning),
and when a man asks,
                    "wanna dance?"
she shrugs, indifferent assent,
and moves her lovely ass.

now appearing

in this photograph
we appear as
"the virgin and the gypsy",
a carnival act,
curious mismatch
of innocence and knowledge.

it is true
i was untouched too long
and too long could not focus
on my centre, the source
and force of hunger . . .

and it is true
you have journeyed far
in caravan
(menagerie, ménages-à-trois,
à quatre, à cinq),
journeyed alone,
performed tricks,
were cunning and wise,
thighs opened, roads,
(till now) you always escaped.

but this is not mismatch,
is not curious:

for what is a gypsy
without his virgin?

42

and what is a virgin alone?

. . . and now we arrive
in the camera's eye,
in a future
even you could not see:
this bare prison yard,
one gypsy, one virgin,
stars grind /
          opposites
embrace.

prison after noon

we move towards the end
of summer,
and the sky above,
flawless, tranquil
as a pool,
immeasurably deep
and far,
reflecting /
                receiving
nothing,
being simply there,

we sit upon the earth,
the yielding grass, we
sit together
with your friends,
3 men (who murdered)
in the sun,
our theme, transcendence,
art.

and when the photographer
(among us) shoots me
once,   twice,
and then again,
i view him backwards
through the lens:
he is forever held.

he is the sort of man
i have observed
walking down yorkville,
a week-day afternoon,
dark hair, dark glasses,
beard, nikon loaded,
at the ready,
waiting for some scene,

i would like to think
his crime an accident,
that he was drunk
                 or stoned,

the way he stands,
his aim is certain /
                 his beauty,

and i smile.

this hand

this hand
familiar with guns
and knives,
the thighs of eager virgins,

this hand
has written poetry,

this hand
was torn and bled,

this
is the hand
that killed a man,

now lies
upon my breast:

      fingers grasping,
      thumb opposed,
      neuron impulse,
      muscle, bone . . .

the sum
of all you've lived
and done,

soul-shuddering,
my lust.

lock-up

treat a man
        like an animal,
and he becomes one:
you know that cornered
instinct to survive,
when time is doing you,
parole board says no.

air canada flies
a fellow inmate home,
another jumps the wall,
years pass,
        they come
and go.

eleven o'clock:

and all along the range
of cells
echoing lock-up,
heart clenched,
steel.

night thoughts

you wait for silence:
one moment,
muffled coughing cease,
one moment,
hand beneath the sheets,
moan suspended,
breath suspended,
there . . .

they are there,
even now as all men sleep
(vulnerable,
                    unwatching),
even now, rhythmic pulsing,
other lives intruding.

inhale, exhale, memory,
desire,
play back /
                    go forward,
anywhere but here:

(here where every man
is jonah,
swallowed whole
and waiting,

here where every man
is street-wise,

48

cocky, treacherous,
lonely and alone).

so dream your world of women,
soft skin whispering warm,
dream fields and seas
and yielding thighs,
mountains to climb
and climb.

kisses, old and new

open i am
open to you

you kiss and
i would arc
upward
at the first thrust

i remain still
surface calm

i betray nothing

i trace the line
of scars
along your tongue

you claim
that other tongue
equally well worn

for each scar
there is a story

tell me
i want to know

there was the lady you fucked dog-style
chill long nights beneath the stars
and you'd come howling at the moon
the moon forever deaf to ecstasy

and there was the lady who loved jazz
the stereo blasting you lay between her thighs
and blew a run of high rippling notes
sent her shuddering head to toe

forever it echoes

in prison
one does not forget

one remembers

and i dream of a man
who once was free
a man will be free again

and i would make of myself
a gift but the gift
remains forbidden

but for now

take this mouth
this greedy mouth
this wicked greedy woman's mouth

parted lips
             a taste of then

strip search

i

i do not like to think of
what happens   when you leave
when the heavy wooden double doors
swing closed behind you

when i cannot see

when they lead you
off into some private
space   have you undress

(here is where your power lies
and here where most vulnerable

thy tender and subversive parts
fur   tissue   muscle)

men don't care
about such things

i care

i register intrusion

ii

i do not like to think of
afterwards and all the days
between visits   when you follow
your course through corridors   when you

are stopped   questioned
proceed   when you greet men
who may be friends

who may be lethal

you wear your body
                          tentatively

caged   monitored
always under threat
this flesh not quite yours
but something to protect

i do not like to think of
when i am not there

when i cannot see

dream

day of unrelenting
sun   california
blue and gold
i browse
among the candles
clothes
in the shelter
of your store
a tourist
only looking

i choose
retire to the room
oval mirror
curtain   chair
undress to music
incense-air

lace scratches
across creamy flesh
i fasten hooks
and you appear

and here is where
my magic fails
i cannot see
what happens next
to love you free
to love you quick

anonymous need
easy access

but here is where
my magic fails
though shadows meet
upon the wall
two bodies stand
quite still

the flood

we file in slowly
one   by   one
our men are waiting
and already it has begun
to rain
yes this is the way
                    the world ends
there is thunder

i wish it would end
here
while we visit
                    watch the clock

see

the electricity goes first
— it always does —
and then the men and women
and all their social systems
till this is no longer prison
and we are not afraid

we share our food /
                    we couple
everyone is equal
our domain is not divided
into the keepers and the kept

we do not know
whether we shall survive
or what inherit

but we are moving
at last

honeymoon

you wrote the script,
you star, direct,
i accept the role,
uncertain
of the shooting date,
uncertain of location:

the falls of niagara,
thousand islands
(always american side),
that new england inn
with atlantic view,
the fireplace
                    and four-poster bed,
never enough of you . . .

you promise the best
loving i've ever had,
we'll eat oysters
and drink champagne,
sea-mist in our hair,
sand in the crotch,
behind rocks,
                    our secluded beach.

only one month,
but a month is enough,
and schedules have to be set,
you're drawn to the sea,

freedom and space,
and i belong to the north.

and it ends
when you put me
                on the train,
and i have to
gaze out the window,

when motion begins,
you on the landing
(another hollywood echo),

but the man
                on the landing,
static and stern,
no reprieve,
                no shouting:
i love you.

you say i must cry
(then)
or spoil the scene,

it has to be romantic.

for you

i am
the throbbing
of one raw nerve

i am
cavity-ache
shaft   tip of desire

i am
vessel-hunger
vessel-thirst

i am
earth-need
earth-embrace

concave
to   convex
your

your supplement
your complement

all science
and logic attest
to the necessity
of you and me

i am nourishment

i am life

cinéma vérité

i would go in
with camera, lights, crew,
through gates electronic,
past robot guards,

i'd transform joyceville
into microcosmic
all-the-world's-a-stage
event,

i'd film the cages,
maze of corridors,
uniformed precision,
clockwork ritual of days,

i'd show boredom,
desperation, violent eruption,
tyranny and pain,

hit men, pushers, indians,
students and embezzlers,
horny strutting queens,

and everyone would start
performing,
and you, presenting
profile

(and i, observer altering
behavior of observed):

there would be chaos,
anarchy,
though perfectly contained.

touching

beneath your open hand,
my body is a map
spread out upon a table.

a map is a key
to the future,
a map is a tool,
a promise.

consider those first explorers
whose ships traced
their way along uncertain coasts,
who with pen and ink
carefully filled in the blanks,
voyaging, recording.

smooth this map,
my body, with your fingertips,
seek out her subtle inlets,
hidden lakes.

rehearse your course:

from hair scandinavian,
eyes blue as ice,
proceeding southward
to cities exotic,
casablanca, marakesh.

rapunzel

today i play
rapunzel,

the only game
i know,

dwelling
in my ivory tower,

in hostile city
confined

(the hourglass
is broken,

mirror on the wall,

jagged edge
meets
jagged edge,

but nothing
seems to hold),

growing hair,

and waiting,

66

the only game
i know.

the cure

did we choose
tragedy
in the beginning?

were we chosen?

did you always bear
the mark of cain?

and will you soon
be free to live?

my mother free
from pain?

i travel your corridors,
sealed, clinical, clean,
it is like an asylum
(hospital, chronic care),
where the cure is
not a cure,
but a warehoused
limbo-life where years
are short as days,
and days as long as nights.

at the bedside
of my mother,
where my mother dies,
cancer in her growing,
malignant, evil, live,

i am watching and recording,
touching, still alone,

boundary
of self and other,

suffering excludes.

at the bedside
of my mother,

in the prison
visiting room,

i would make love
with you,
i would defy
the dying force,
eros conquering
thanatos,
triumph of the flesh.

69

headlines

sunday morning
at breakfast
autumn 1976:

"riot at joyceville",
over the wires comes
the news,
a riot at your prison,
"order is restored,
the convicts are subdued."

by guns?   gas?
promises?
method never mentioned,
cause is not established /
           no casualties are listed,
and from all accounts
— the warden's press release —
one cannot tell
how serious it is,
this could be attica or less.

i feel like a woman whose
man is at the front,
and who, hearing
of defeat,
must wait,

and as i wait,
there are no bandages to roll,
no veterans to visit,
to take on walks through hospital
grounds, to read to
or write letters

("when the boys come home again . . ."
no songs of solace).

good and evil,
god and country,
these absolutes do not exist:

the enemy is undefined,
uncertain lines are drawn.

another week:

another uprising
in new westminster,
in quebec,
they're burning laval.

again   almost

light through white
gauze curtains,
brass bed gleaming,
woman awakening,
softly
            unfurling
                        to morning

(again   almost
dreamed
you into flesh:
mouth-taste,
curve of belly,

and now wrapping thighs
round memory of),

warm sun,

you haunt my room.

picture it

i

picture me
mary steinhauser,

picture you
andy bruce,

and so do headline heroes
reveal us to ourselves.

ii

i have pored over their smudgy
photograph, always the same
photograph, posed for
at a prison dance,
reproduced in newspapers,
proof.

anywhere else
an ordinary couple:

a man, big as a bear
and handsome, one protective
arm drawn around his woman's
shoulder.

73

she seems happy,
occupies her space in the photo-
graph, her place beside him,
comfortably, almost
assertive:

> *it may be prison*
> *but this moment*
> *where i want to be*

(later she confessed
she feared
for andy and herself.)

iii

picture it:

to pass through those grinding
gates every day,
to confront the machinery
of men,
to know that inside
and out,
there is a cycle
one cannot argue,
alter.

to begin optimistically
and watch hope
worn away,

to find a man worth saving
(though saving's not the word),
to compromise,
to console with smiles,
with brush of flesh,
the painkiller
not the cure . . .

iv

i could have been
your mary,

i could have been
their con-lover,
bleeding heart,

we could have met
in my office,
and on government desk,
among forms and memos,
private files,

bodies joined
in subversive dance.

V

i have heard
they are making a movie
of steinhauser/bruce,

perhaps
they will make one
of us:

may they make it
hollywood, make it slick,
a film without end
or filmed with mercy,
freeze frame before
                        bullets begin.

release

i construct the bridge,
smooth arcs and parallel lines
(all must be right),
degrees of angles,
                    lengths of steel,
firmbalanced between
here   and   there.

i construct the bridge
until finally
it is more than symbol,
until finally
i see the perfect
sweep of sky, and below,
there is the lake
and a thousand green islands,
dazzling . . .

and suddenly the car.

you are escorted
by two mounties, wooden,
obvious in plainclothes
(hollywood:
strictly grade b),
they let you off
where the bridge begins,
and watch:

you walk with purpose
(the sun at your left),
knowing every step
is away,

and even knowing
i am at the end
                of the bridge,
and waiting,
you do not run.

the hostage

i have adopted
strange habits,

i carve miniature
guns
out of ivory soap,

i secrete still-wrapped
blades
in vagina,

i collect clippings,
confused accounts,
prison escapes,
hostage dramas.

i am grown morbid
with lust /
         passion
never far from blood.

over and over,
i rehearse the scene:

your sudden burst of heroics
(nothing left to lose),
the waiting, watching guards,
my tender flesh between,

and again we make it
to the highway,
the abandoned car
(warm, narcotic odour,
bodies pressed to leather),
forget to drive away.

only here

only here have i
seen you
(perhaps mirage),
and only
in these clothes:

and so i dress you
in leather, fur,
velvet, suede,
shirt white satin
slashed to waist,
silver finger-rings,
chains of gold . . .

sounds like penthouse/viva
vision,

slick fantasied,
soft focus,

and i dream
of vaseline on lens,
and other tricks with flesh.

chastity

enforced
our chastity,

anachronistic,

chivalry and honour,

you, the knight,
i, the flower,

untrammelled
and untouched.

how long desire
without release,

how long unsatisfied:

to feel you
at my centre
thrust
        then calm,

to be finally
(for you) woman
warm-enfolding
man . . .

and still,
in our waiting-
visiting-room,

another year,
i watch the clock:

your mouth
tastes of metal,

i grow moist,

stubborn my flesh,
          its blind response.

svengali

i

subtle hands,
magnetic eyes,
you are
a practised showman:

i believe
you could
saw beautiful women
in half,

you could
extort fortunes
from lonely widows

(lotions, potions, soothing
words, the magic tip
of your tongue),

more than illusion,
will, design,

you have confessed
your godliness.

ii

and i, who was so easy,
easier than the rest,

i was waiting all along
to be freed by master-touch:

sitting
in a darkened room
nursing dying mother,

lying
in a darkened room
for men to leave and enter.

iii

i have made you
bad man,
made you good,

i have yielded
a thousand nights,

a thrust
is a thrust
and power, my love,

i have tasted
my own sweet blood,

and always
the poem taking shape,

and always
desire and doubt.

iv

some women
will do anything,
held in suspense
by a promise,

some women
will do anything
to serve a god
or devil,

to court the source
of life and death,

your captive,

roles reverse.

86

V

but if the bad man
is a myth
(celluloid and soundtrack),

and if this lady poet
was only hungry
for her subject,

and hungry
for more savage cock,

and hungry
for the drama,

when art becomes confused
with life,
and power is a game,

i dream you
in me to the hilt,

crime,
        aphrodisiac.